MAR      2019

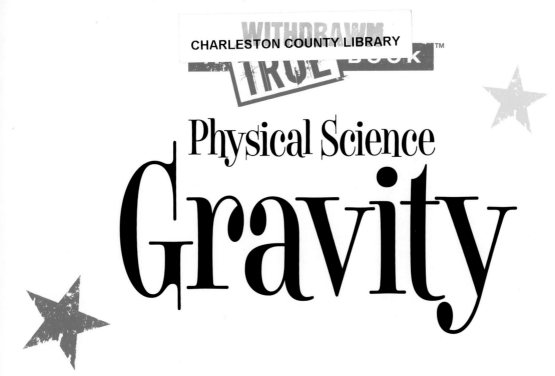

TRUE BOOK™

# Physical Science
# Gravity

A L E X A   K U R Z I U S

**Children's Press®**
An Imprint of Scholastic Inc.

**Content Consultant**
Valarie Akerson, PhD, Professor of Science Education
Department of Curriculum and Instruction
Indiana University Bloomington, Bloomington, Indiana

Library of Congress Cataloging-in-Publication Data
Names: Kurzius, Alexa, author.
Title: Gravity / By Alexa Kurzius.
Description: New York, NY : Children's Press, an imprint of Scholastic Inc., 2019. | Series: A true book |
    Includes bibliographical references and index.
Identifiers: LCCN 2018034484| ISBN 9780531131398 (library binding) | ISBN 9780531136027 (pbk.)
Subjects:  LCSH: Gravity—Juvenile literature.
Classification: LCC QC178 .K973 2019 | DDC 531/.14—dc23
LC record available at https://lccn.loc.gov/2018034484

All rights reserved. Published in 2019 by Children's Press, an imprint of Scholastic Inc.
Printed in North Mankota, MN, USA  113

SCHOLASTIC, CHILDREN'S PRESS, A TRUE BOOK™, and associated logos are trademarks and/or
registered trademarks of Scholastic Inc.

Scholastic Inc., 557 Broadway, New York, NY 10012

1 2 3 4 5 6 7 8 9 10 R 28 27 26 25 24 23 22 21 20 19

**Front cover: Skydivers**
**Back cover: A competitor in the luge event**

# Find the Truth!

**Everything** you are about to read is true *except* for one of the sentences on this page.

Which one is **TRUE**?

**T or F**  Gravity exists only on Earth.

**T or F**  Scientists are still learning new things about gravity.

Find the answers in this book.

# Contents

THE **BIG** TRUTH!

## Living in Zero Gravity

Military fighter jet

**Sir Isaac Newton**

5

# Think About It!

Closely examine the photo to the left. What do you notice about the image? What ideas do you have that might explain what's going on in the photo? Once you have some guesses about what is happening, try to think about *why* it's happening.

## Stumped?

Want to know more? Turn the page!

# Without Gravity, We'd Float Away

A floating astronaut is not the product of a magic trick. It is what happens when there is practically zero **gravity**.

When outside their spaceship, astronauts use jet packs to control where they travel. Or they tie themselves to their spacecraft so they don't drift away, which would be dangerous. Inside a spacecraft, astronauts spend a lot of their time floating freely.

Astronauts float freely inside the International Space Station.

Talented skateboarders can do jumps and other tricks even as gravity pulls them toward the ground.

Gravity is one of the most important forces in the universe. It's invisible, but it's vital to our existence. Without it, everything would float like astronauts do in space.

Gravity is the pull of one object upon another. Earth's gravity, for example, pulls objects toward its center. But does gravity behave differently with different objects? Does a heavier object fall faster than a lighter one? Turn to page 40 to do a short activity.

The farther objects are from one another, the less powerful the gravitational pull is.

Ropes, pulleys, and other equipment help keep a rock climber safe during a climb.

# CHAPTER 1

# Understanding Gravity

On Earth, gravity is a force that pulls all objects toward the center of Earth. It's why items fall to the ground.

Rock climbers know this. They work against gravity when they attempt a difficult climb. They work with gravity when they come down. They use a strong rope and a harnass to carefully lower themselves to the ground.

Everything you see— and even what you don't see—in this photo is made up of matter.

# Gravity Between Objects

Heavier objects have more gravity. But why is that? The answer comes down to the amount of **matter** in an object.

All objects are made up of matter. Some matter you can see. Other matter you can't see because it's too small. Atoms and molecules are some of the smallest examples. All matter is made up of atoms and molecules.

**Mass** measures how much matter an object contains. The heavier the object, the more mass it has. The more mass it has, the more gravity it has.

Earth is heavier than you can imagine. That's why we are pulled toward Earth. (We have a comparatively tiny amount of gravity ourselves!) But the heaviest object in our solar system is the sun. Its gravity causes every planet in our solar system to **orbit**, or move around, it.

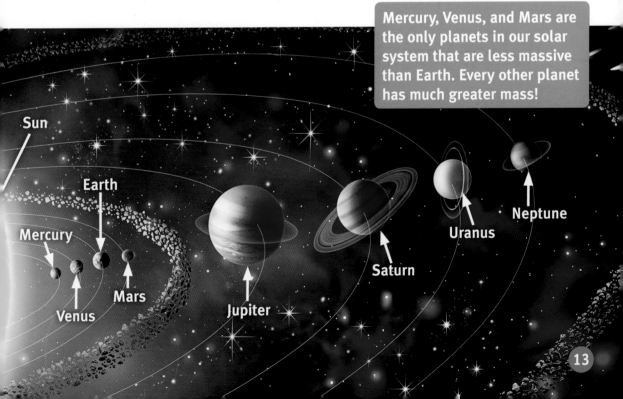

Mercury, Venus, and Mars are the only planets in our solar system that are less massive than Earth. Every other planet has much greater mass!

Sun

Earth

Mercury

Mars

Venus

Jupiter

Saturn

Uranus

Neptune

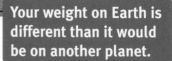

Your weight on Earth is different than it would be on another planet.

# Weight Versus Mass

**Weight** measures how much gravity pulls on an object. It's different from mass.

Objects fall at a constant speed over a period of time, as long as no other force, like wind, acts on them. On Earth, this is about 32 feet (9.8 meters) per second squared. Weight is the mass of an object multiplied by this constant speed.

# Early Ideas About Gravity

In ancient times, people thought Earth was the center of the universe. These ideas about gravity would change in time. Astronomers and mathematicians began to use **data** to develop a better understanding of our solar system.

Nicolaus Copernicus was a Polish astronomer in the 1500s. He used observations to show that the planets in our solar system orbit the sun.

Copernicus's diagram of the universe showed the sun at the center.

# Is Earth the Center?

Tycho Brahe, a Danish astronomer, was skeptical of Copernicus's ideas. So he recorded data on how the planets moved.

Brahe gave his data to his assistant, Johannes Kepler. The German astronomer used the data to show that planets move in an oval shape around the sun. This shape is called an **ellipse**. Kepler's explanation blended math and astronomy to explain how planets move through space.

Tycho Brahe's data was incredibly accurate, which allowed Johannes Kepler to make detailed studies of the planets' orbits.

# Galileo and His Work

Italian astronomer Galileo Galilei thought Copernicus was right. Galileo made telescopes in the 1600s that could help someone see how planets moved. He used the telescopes to

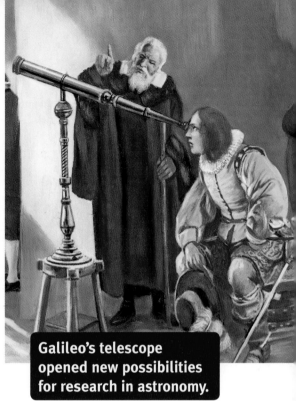

Galileo's telescope opened new possibilities for research in astronomy.

observe the planet Venus. He noted it has phases, just like Earth's moon. He also recorded data about the locations of stars in the sky. With this data, he argued that Copernicus was correct that the sun was the center of the universe. Scientists in future centuries eventually determined that the sun is the center of our solar system, but not the whole universe.

Galileo was put on trial for his scientific arguments, which went against the Catholic Church's teachings.

Galileo published his work in 1623. It angered the Catholic Church, which had a lot of power at the time. They arrested and tried Galileo, and imprisoned him in his home for the rest of his life.

During this time, Galileo continued to study. He focused on falling objects. As objects fall, they experience resistance from the air they're traveling through. Galileo wrote that, without this air resistance, all objects fall at the same speed no matter what they weigh.

# Developing a Theory

In the end, it was Sir Isaac Newton who developed a **theory** about gravity in the late 1600s. Newton was an English mathematician. He told friends that one day he was sitting under an apple tree when an apple fell on his head. This made him wonder about the force that caused the apple to fall. Was it the same force that made the moon orbit Earth? In 1687, Newton published *Principia*, which summarized his ideas.

Sir Isaac Newton made ground-breaking discoveries about gravity, light and color, motion, and math.

Earth

The moon

Tides are caused by the moon's pull on Earth's water.

## Newton Defines Gravity

Newton wrote that a force called gravity exists between any two objects in the universe. It becomes weaker as objects move farther apart. Gravity is stronger for objects with more mass and weaker for objects with less mass.

He also described the motion of the planets. This proved that the works of Kepler and Galileo were correct. Newton even explained that high and low tides are caused by the gravities of Earth and the moon.

# Newton's Laws

Gravity and Newton's laws of motion are what make this device, called Newton's Cradle, work.

Newton came up with three laws of motion.

They are still used today:

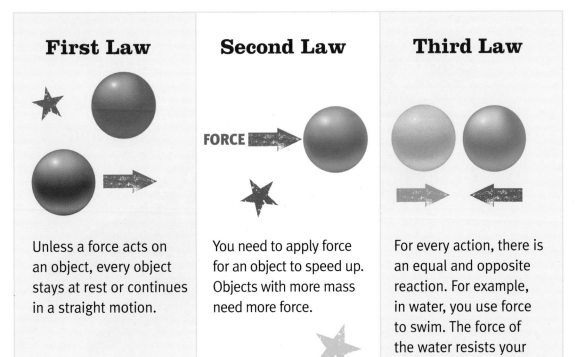

### First Law

Unless a force acts on an object, every object stays at rest or continues in a straight motion.

### Second Law

FORCE

You need to apply force for an object to speed up. Objects with more mass need more force.

### Third Law

For every action, there is an equal and opposite reaction. For example, in water, you use force to swim. The force of the water resists your movement.

A luge athlete speeds down a track at up to 90 miles (145 km) per hour on a tiny sled with no brakes!

An athlete from Canada competes in the luge event at the 2006 Olympics.

# CHAPTER 2

# Extreme Gravity on Earth

Luge is one of the most popular Winter Olympic sports. Athletes can rocket down an icy track at extreme speeds. Gravity is a big reason they go so fast. The track is on a steep incline, and ice has little **friction**. So the sled quickly accelerates, or speeds up.

Accelerating quickly places an incredible gravitational force on the body. This is the force that keeps you on Earth. It is typically measured in the unit g, for gravity.

Sparks fly as a Formula One car speeds down the track.

# G Forces

Most of the time on Earth, we experience 1 g. But certain extreme activities are different. They cause a person to experience more g forces. Have you ever ridden a roller coaster? As you make a fast turn, you feel yourself pulled against your seat. That means you're feeling more g's. The greater the g force, the greater the pull of gravity and the heavier you feel.

# Greatest G Forces on Earth

What are some ways people feel more gravity without ever leaving the planet? Here are just a few examples.

**Military fighter jet**
9g

**Rocket launch**
3.5g

**Formula One race car**
6g

**Luge sled**
5g

**Normal gravity on Earth**
1g

Albert Einstein was a physics professor in Germany until he moved to the United States in 1933.

Before leaving Germany permanently and moving to New Jersey, Albert Einstein visited Pasadena, California, in 1931.

# CHAPTER 3

# Putting Theories Together

For nearly 200 years, Newton's laws of gravity remained unchanged. But sometimes his work did not make sense. Atoms and other tiny objects did not always follow the rules. Even the planet Mercury didn't move as Newton's laws predicted. Then Albert Einstein came along. He was one of the most influential thinkers of the 20th century. His theories about gravity, light, and space would change how people view the world and the universe.

# Adjusting the Rules

Einstein revised Newton's laws on gravity. He said that massive objects, such as planets and stars, bend space. As a result, other objects can move around them. Einstein also said that gravity affects particles that don't have mass, such as light.

Einstein's work helped us understand black holes too. These are objects in space created when a massive star dies. Black holes are so **dense** and have so much gravity that light cannot escape.

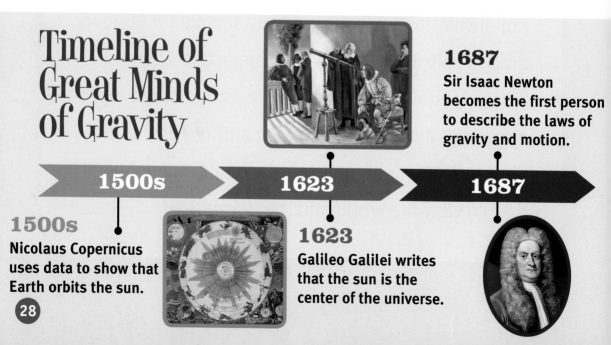

# Timeline of Great Minds of Gravity

**1500s**
Nicolaus Copernicus uses data to show that Earth orbits the sun.

**1623**
Galileo Galilei writes that the sun is the center of the universe.

**1687**
Sir Isaac Newton becomes the first person to describe the laws of gravity and motion.

1500s → 1623 → 1687

When Einstein was alive, no one had developed technology to observe some of his ideas. But technology has caught up. Scientists built special **observatories** in Louisiana and Washington. They began collecting data in 1999.

In 2015, researchers heard a signal from two colliding black holes 7 trillion miles (11 trillion km) away. The event was so intense it created curves, or "gravity waves," in the fabric of space. This supported Einstein's work.

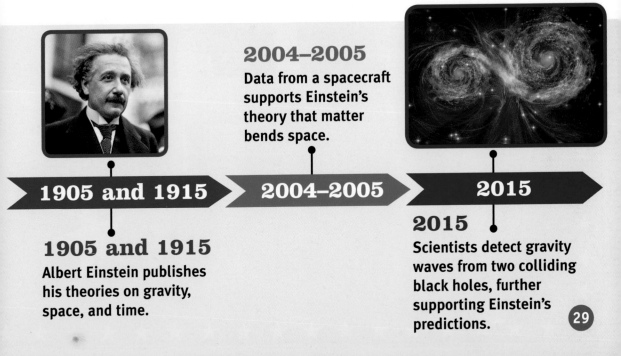

**2004–2005**
Data from a spacecraft supports Einstein's theory that matter bends space.

**1905 and 1915**

**2004–2005**

**2015**

**1905 and 1915**
Albert Einstein publishes his theories on gravity, space, and time.

**2015**
Scientists detect gravity waves from two colliding black holes, further supporting Einstein's predictions.

# Living in Zero Gravity

Everything floats in space. It takes some getting used to. The International Space Station (ISS) orbits Earth and experiences almost zero gravity. Read on to learn some of the ways this affects the people onboard.

Astronauts live there and conduct research. They catch floating food and liquid in their mouths. They use a tube for the toilet, and they strap themselves to a wall to sleep.

It might seem fun, but weightlessness takes a toll. Muscles and bones weaken. Astronauts use bikes and treadmills to stay in shape.

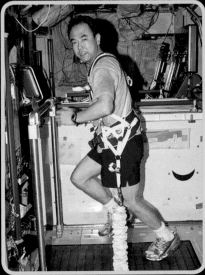

On Earth, scientists are studying how living in space affects health. That's so they can plan safe, longer space missions. One of these studies compared Mark and Scott Kelly, who are U.S. astronauts and twins. Mark spent more than 50 days in space during his career. But Scott spent a record of 520 days there. One long mission lasted almost a year, the longest any American had lived in space.

Scott experienced some changes in his health while in space. But over time back on Earth, his health returned to normal.

A total of 12 people have walked on the moon.

Astronaut John Young demonstrates an easy leap in the air as he salutes the U.S. flag on the moon in 1972.

# CHAPTER 4

# Gravity in Space

Astronaut Neil Armstrong first walked on the moon in 1969. His first steps were kind of bouncy. That's because the moon has only one-sixth the gravity of Earth. The moon is a natural satellite. It orbits around Earth because of Earth's gravity.

Armstrong knew what he was getting into. He and other astronauts had trained in low-gravity environments to prepare for their missions.

Astronauts float for a few seconds on the Vomit Comet (left). The Vomit Comet plane dives toward Earth (below).

# All Aboard the Vomit Comet

Beginning in the 1950s, NASA (National Aeronautics and Space Administration) used a research plane to train astronauts. Team members called the plane the Vomit Comet. It flew up and down in an arc. Passengers felt different levels of gravity at different points. For about 15 to 25 seconds at the top of the arc, they felt almost zero gravity. Everything floated. The Vomit Comet flew 30 to 40 arcs each flight. Some astronauts got pretty sick!

To leave Earth, airplanes must overcome two forces: gravity and drag. Airplanes are very heavy. Remember, weight is the force of gravity. It pulls the plane downward. The plane's powerful engines create thrust, pushing the plane forward. As the plane moves forward, air resistance causes drag, pushing against the plane. As the plane speeds up, it lifts off the ground. Lift pushes the plane up. In an airplane takeoff, thrust must be greater than drag and lift must be greater than weight.

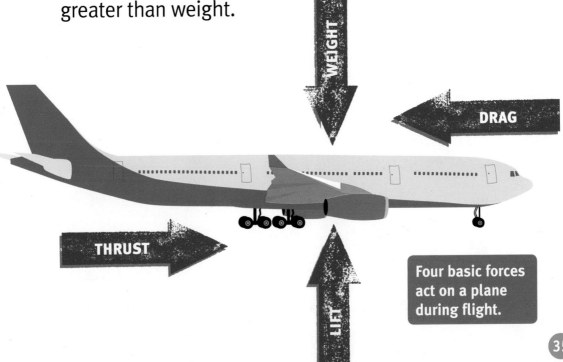

WEIGHT

DRAG

THRUST

LIFT

Four basic forces act on a plane during flight.

Up to this point, astronauts have only orbited Earth and visited the moon. But someday, they might visit Mars.

Mars is completely different from Earth. A year there lasts 687 days compared to Earth's 365 days. There's no oxygen to breathe. Dust storms can cover the planet and last for months. Also, gravity is about half of what it is on Earth. That's because the planet is smaller and farther from the sun.

Astronauts on Mars will have to adjust to living with lower gravity.

# Gravity and Mars Rovers

Though humans haven't made it to Mars yet, spacecraft have. Robots called rovers explore the planet, taking photographs and collecting rock

The *Curiosity* rover landed on Mars in 2012.

samples. The images and data are sent back to Earth for scientists to study.

Mars's rovers have a machine called an accelerometer. It measures forces such as gravity. The accelerometer tells the rover which way is down and helps it move. On Earth, vehicles such as ships and trains use accelerometers too.

# Space and the Future

People who study Mars exploration think about gravity every day. But plenty of other people think about gravity to do their jobs too. Take a look at the sidebar on page 39 for some examples.

Today, we know gravity is a force acting on all objects in the universe. It's why objects fall to the ground on Earth and why planets orbit the sun. But people are still asking questions and learning new things about gravity. Maybe someday, you could make the next big discovery! ★

Do you want to explore space someday?

# STEM Careers

There are many jobs that involve gravity. Here are just a few:

- **Aerospace engineers** design airplanes and spacecraft.
- **Airplane pilots** work with gravity to fly and land planes safely.
- **Mathematicians** create and improve theories of gravity with equations.
- **Mechanical engineers** consider gravity when designing and building tools and machines.
- **Physicists** study gravity to learn about our universe.
- **Race car engineers** design cars to speed along tracks and battle intense gravitational forces.
- **Science writers** explain gravity and other scientific concepts to their readers.

- **Spacecraft designers** think about how gravity differs depending on where the vehicles travel.

DRAWING OF A ROCKET

90516

# How Does Gravity Work?

Some objects are heavier than others. Does this weight matter when objects fall?

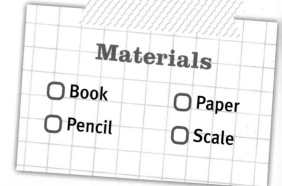

## Materials

- ☐ Book
- ☐ Pencil
- ☐ Paper
- ☐ Scale

## Directions

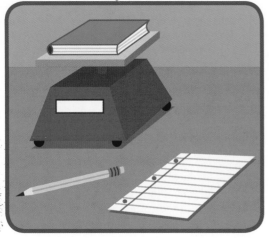

My Prediction

I Think...

**1.** Weigh the book and then the pencil on the scale. Record the weight of each object.

**2.** Make a prediction. Which item do you think will fall to the ground first? Write down your idea.

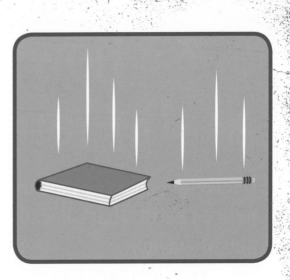

**3.** Hold one object in each hand. Make sure the objects are the same distance from the ground.

**4.** Drop the objects. Which one hit the ground first?

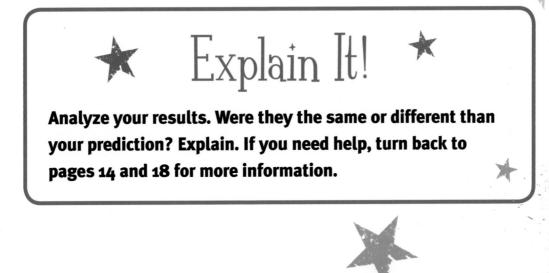

# Explain It!

Analyze your results. Were they the same or different than your prediction? Explain. If you need help, turn back to pages 14 and 18 for more information.

# How Much Do You Weigh?

Our weight on other planets is a fraction of what we weigh here on Earth. That's because each planet has a different pull of gravity.

We can figure out how much we would weigh on another planet with the following equation:

$$\text{Weight on Earth} \times \frac{\text{Gravity on other planet relative to Earth}}{} = \text{Weight on that planet}$$

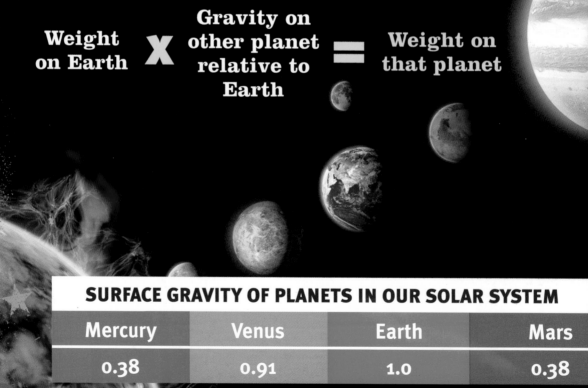

### SURFACE GRAVITY OF PLANETS IN OUR SOLAR SYSTEM

| Mercury | Venus | Earth | Mars |
|---------|-------|-------|------|
| 0.38 | 0.91 | 1.0 | 0.38 |

## Example
**The moon has 0.16 the gravity of Earth. What would a 100-pound (45.4-kilogram) person weigh on the moon?**

Set up an equation and solve. You can use pounds:

**100 pounds ✕ 0.16 ═ 16 pounds**

Or you can use kilograms:

**45.4 kilograms ✕ 0.16 ═ 7.3 kilograms**

Either way, that person weighs a lot less on the moon than on Earth!

Use this equation and the chart below to find out how much you would weigh on each planet in our solar system.

| Jupiter | Saturn | Uranus | Neptune |
|---------|--------|--------|---------|
| 2.34 | 0.93 | 0.92 | 1.12 |

## True Statistics

**Acceleration of falling objects due to Earth's gravity:** 32.2 ft/sec² (9.8 m/sec²)

**Weight of a 100-pound (45.4 kg) person on the moon:** 16 lb. (7.3 kg)

**Weight of a 100-pound (45.4 kg) person on the sun:** 2,707 lb. (1,228 kg)

**Speed of light:** 186,282 mi./sec (299,792 km/sec)

**Number of objects larger than a softball orbiting Earth:** More than 8,000

**Mass of the sun compared to the mass of Earth:** 333,000 times greater than Earth

**Mass of the moon compared to the mass of Earth:** 0.0123 times the size of Earth

## Did you find the truth?

**F** Gravity exists only on Earth.

**T** Scientists are still learning new things about gravity.

# Resources

## Books

Berne, Jennifer. *On a Beam of Light: A Story of Albert Einstein*. San Francisco: Chronicle Books, 2016.

Boothroyd, Jennifer. *What Holds Us to Earth? A Look at Gravity*. Minneapolis: Lerner Classroom, 2011.

Chin, Jason. *Gravity*. New York: Roaring Brook Press, 2014.

Pohlen, Jerome. *Albert Einstein and Relativity for Kids: His Life and Ideas With 21 Activities and Thought Experiments*. Chicago: Chicago Review Press, 2012.

**Visit this Scholastic website for more information on gravity:**
★ www.factsfornow.scholastic.com
Enter the keyword **Gravity**

# Important Words

**data** (DAY-tuh) information collected in a place so that something can be done with it

**dense** (DENS) heavy for an object's size. Density is a measure of an object's mass compared to its size.

**ellipse** (ih-LIPS) a flat, oval shape

**friction** (FRIK-shun) the force that slows down objects when they rub against each other

**gravity** (GRAV-ih-tee) the force that pulls objects toward one another and keeps them from floating away

**mass** (MAS) the amount of physical matter that an object contains

**matter** (MAT-ur) something that has weight and takes up space, such as a solid, liquid, or gas

**observatories** (uhb-ZURV-uh-tor-eez) buildings or places designed to observe the universe

**orbit** (OR-bit) the curved path followed by a moon, planet, or satellite as it circles another planet or the sun

**theory** (THEER-ee) an idea or set of ideas that explains how or why something happens

**weight** (WATE) a calculation that measures the pull of gravity on an object

# Index

Page numbers in **bold** indicate illustrations.

# About the Author

Alexa Kurzius writes and produces videos for Scholastic's elementary STEM magazines. She's been reporting ever since the fourth grade, when she penned a picture book about penguins. She has an undergraduate degree in English and psychology and a master's degree in science journalism. She lives in New York City with her husband.

**PHOTOGRAPHS** ©: cover: Digital Vision/Getty Images; back cover: Clive Mason/Getty Images; 3: SuperStock/ Science Faction Images/age fotostock; 4: rusm/Getty Images; 5 top: NASA/Johnson Space Center/Science Source; 5 bottom: IanDagnall Computing/Alamy Images; 6-7: Science Source/NASA/Getty Images; 8: NASA/ Johnson Space Center/Science Source; 9: Tom Dunkley/Getty Images; 10-11: Fernando Nuñez/EyeEm/Getty Images; 12: William D. Bachman/Science Source; 13: BSIP/UIG/Getty Images; 14: Peter Dazeley/Getty Images; 15: Pictures From History/The Image Works; 16: Transcendental Graphics/Getty Images; 17: Bettmann/Getty Images; 18: Leemage/Corbis/Getty Images; 19: IanDagnall Computing/Alamy Images; 20: SuperStock/Science Faction Images/age fotostock; 21 top: Jojje/Shutterstock; 21 center: Glinskaja Olga/Shutterstock; 22-23: Clive Mason/Getty Images; 24: Hoch Zwei/picture-alliance/dpa/AP Images; 25 plane: rusm/Getty Images; 25 rocket: Ben Cooper/Superstock, Inc.; 25 car: mirafoto/imageBROKER/Superstock, Inc.; 25 girl: Hans Kim/Shutterstock; 25 luge: imageBROKER/Superstock, Inc.; 25 background: Reid Wiseman/NASA; 26-27: Image courtesy of the Observatories of the Carnegie Institution for Science Collection at the Huntington Library, San Marino, California; 28 left: Pictures From History/The Image Works; 28 center: Bettmann/Getty Images; 28 right: IanDagnall Computing/Alamy Images; 29 left: Library of Congress/Getty Images; 29 right: Stocktrek Images/Superstock, Inc.; 30-31: NASA; 31 top: NASA; 31 right: NASA; 31 bottom: NASA Image Collection/Alamy Images; 32-33: NASA/ Science Source; 34: NC Collections/Alamy Images; 34 inset: NASA Image Collection/Alamy Images; 35: Paola Crash/Shutterstock; 36: MasPix/Alamy Images; 37: Stocktrek Images/Superstock, Inc.; 38: JGI/Jamie Grill/Getty Images; 39: Malchev/Shutterstock; 40-41 illustrations: Danny E. Rivera; 40 paper: billnoll/iStockphoto; 42-43: mkarco/Shutterstock; 44: NASA.